Baby G.

You are the
anár to my fesenjún

Pronunciation Guide©

Persian	English	Pronunciation
اَ	a	**a**nt
آ	á	**a**rm
ب	b	**b**at
د	d	**d**og
اِ	e	**e**nd
ف	f	**f**un
گ	g	**g**o
ه	h	**h**at
ح	h	**h**at
ی	í	m**ee**t
ج	j	**j**et
ک	k	**k**ey
ل	l	**l**ove
م	m	**m**e
ن	n	**n**ap
اُ	o	**o**n
پ	p	**p**at
ق	q/gh*	me**r**ci
ر	r	**r**un
س	s	**s**un
ص	s	**s**un
ث	s	**s**un

Persian	English	Pronunciation
ت	t	**t**op
ط	t	**t**op
و	ú	m**oo**n
و	v	**v**an
ی	y	**y**es
ذ	z	**z**oo
ز	z	**z**oo
ض	z	**z**oo
ظ	z	**z**oo
چ	**ch**	**ch**air
غ	**gh***	mer**c**i
خ	**kh***	ba**ch**
ش	**sh**	**sh**are
ژ	**zh**	plea**s**ure
ع	'	uh-oh†

*	: guttural sound from back of throat
†	: glottal stop, breathing pause
ّ	: Indicates a double letter
ً	: Indicates the letter n sound
لا	: Indicates combination of letter l & á (lá)
اى	: Indicates the long í sound (ee in m**ee**t)
اِی	: Indicates the long í sound (ee in m**ee**t)
(...)	: Indicates colloquial use

Englisi	Farsi
A a	أَ óÓ ´alef
Á á	آ اا ´alef
B b	ب بیب Be
D d	د دد dál
E e	اِ ◌ِ◌
F f	ف ففف fe
G g	گ گگگ gáf
H h	ه ههه he
H h	ح ححح he
Í í	ی ییی ye
J j	ج ججج jim
K k	ک ککک káf
L l	ل للل lám

Englisi	Farsi
M m	م ممم mím
N n	ن ننن nún
O o	أُ ◌ُ◌
P p	پ پیپ pe
Q q	ق ققق qáf
R r	ر رر re
S s	س سسس sin
S s	ص صصص sád
S s	ث ثثث se
T t	ت تتت te
T t	ط ططط tá
Ú ú	و وو váv
V v	و وو váv

Englisi	Farsi
Y y	ی ییی ye
Z z	ذ ذذ zál
Z z	ز زز ze
Z z	ض ضضض zád
Z z	ظ ظظظ zá
Ch <u>ch</u>	چ ججج <u>che</u>
Gh <u>gh</u>	غ غغغ ghayn
Kh <u>kh</u>	خ خخخ <u>khe</u>
Sh <u>sh</u>	ش ششش <u>shín</u>
Zh <u>zh</u>	ژ ژژ <u>zhe</u>
'	ع ععع ayn

Letter Guide©

غ غغغ

End Ákhar → Middle Vasat ↑ Beginning Aval ↑ Alone Tanhá

The Persian Alphabet

We want to simplify your Persian learning journey as it is such a unique & enigmatic language. There are 32 official Persian letters. The letters change form depending on their position in a word or when they appear separate from other letters. For example, the letter <u>gh</u>ayn غ has four ways of being written depending on where it appears in any given word:

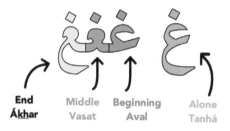

End
Á<u>kh</u>ar

Middle
Vasat

Beginning
Aval

Alone
Tanhá

It is important to note that Persian books are read from right to left (←). There are 7 separate or stand-alone letters that do not connect in the same way to adjacent letters (these will not be depicted in red). They are:

Stand alone
Tanhá vámístan

The short vowels a, e & o are usually omitted in literature and are depicted by markings above & below letters (ﹷ ﹹ). They are not allocated a letter name, unlike their long vowel counterparts á: alef, í: ye & ú: váv (و ی آ).

Apple

Síb

سیب

í: as (ee) in m<u>ee</u>t

Banana

Moz

موز

Mandarin

Nárengí

نارِنگی

á: as (a) in <u>a</u>rm
í: as (ee) in m<u>ee</u>t

Orange

Porteghál

پُرتِقال

á: as (a) in a̲rm

Plum

Álú
آلو

á: as (a) in <u>a</u>rm
ú: as (oo) in m<u>oo</u>n

Peach

Húlú

هُلو

ú: as (oo) in m<u>oo</u>n

Nectarine

Shalíl

شَليل

í: as (ee) in m<u>ee</u>t

Apricot

Zardálú

زَردآلو

á: as (a) in a̲rm
ú: as (oo) in mo̲o̲n

Mango

Anbeh

آنبِه

Watermelon

Hendeváneh

هِنْدِوانِه

(Hendúneh)

á: as (a) in <u>a</u>rm
ú: as (oo) in m<u>oo</u>n

Cherry

Gílás

گیلاس

í: as (ee) in m<u>ee</u>t

á: as (a) in <u>a</u>rm

Pomegranate

Anár

اَنار

á: as (a) in <u>a</u>rm

Lemon

Límú

ليمو

í: as (ee) in m<u>ee</u>t
ú: as (oo) in m<u>oo</u>n

Lime

Límú tor<u>sh</u>

لیمو تُرش

í: as (ee) in m<u>ee</u>t
ú: as (oo) in m<u>oo</u>n

Strawberry

Tútfarangí

توت فَرَنگی

ú: as (oo) in m<u>oo</u>n

í: as (ee) in m<u>ee</u>t

Mulberry

Tút

توت

ú: as (oo) in m<u>oo</u>n

Grape

Angúr

اَنگُور

ú: as (oo) in m<u>oo</u>n

Fig

Anjír

اَنجیر

í: as (ee) in m<u>ee</u>t

Pineapple

Ánánás

آناناس

á: as (a) in <u>a</u>rm

Coconut

Nárgíl

نارگیل

á: as (a) in <u>a</u>rm
í: as (ee) in m<u>ee</u>t

Date

<u>Kh</u>ormá

خُرما

á: as (a) in <u>a</u>rm

Pear

Golábí

گُلابی

á: as (a) in <u>a</u>rm
í: as (ee) in m<u>ee</u>t

Cucumber

<u>Kh</u>íár

خيار

í: as (ee) in m<u>ee</u>t
á: as (a) in <u>a</u>rm

Tomato

Gojeh Farangí

گوجه فَرَنگی

í: as (ee) in m<u>ee</u>t

Olive

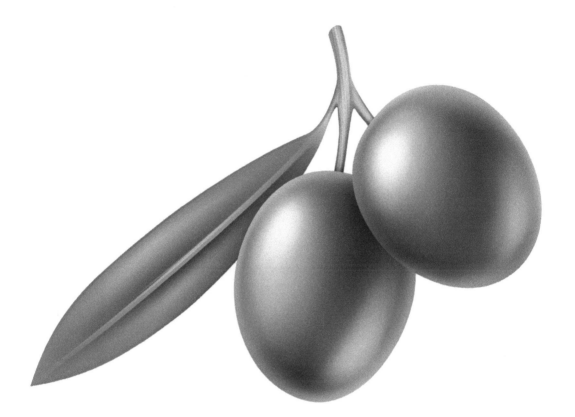

Zeytún

زِيتون

ú: as (oo) in m<u>oo</u>n

Persimmon

<u>K</u>hormálú

خُرمالو

á: as (a) in <u>a</u>rm
ú: as (oo) in m<u>oo</u>n

Cantaloupe

Tálebí

طالِبى

á: as (a) in <u>a</u>rm
í: as (ee) in m<u>ee</u>t

Honeydew

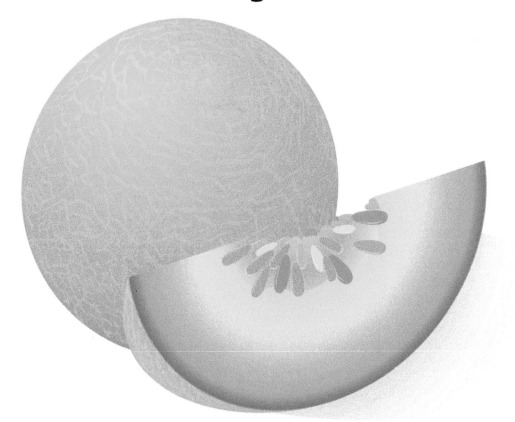

<u>Kh</u>arbúzeh

ú: as (oo) in m<u>oo</u>n

CPSIA information can be obtained
at www.ICGtesting.com
Printed in the USA
BVHW051346211221
624594BV00016B/1432